Nelson Gra~~ Internatio~~

Pupil Book 5

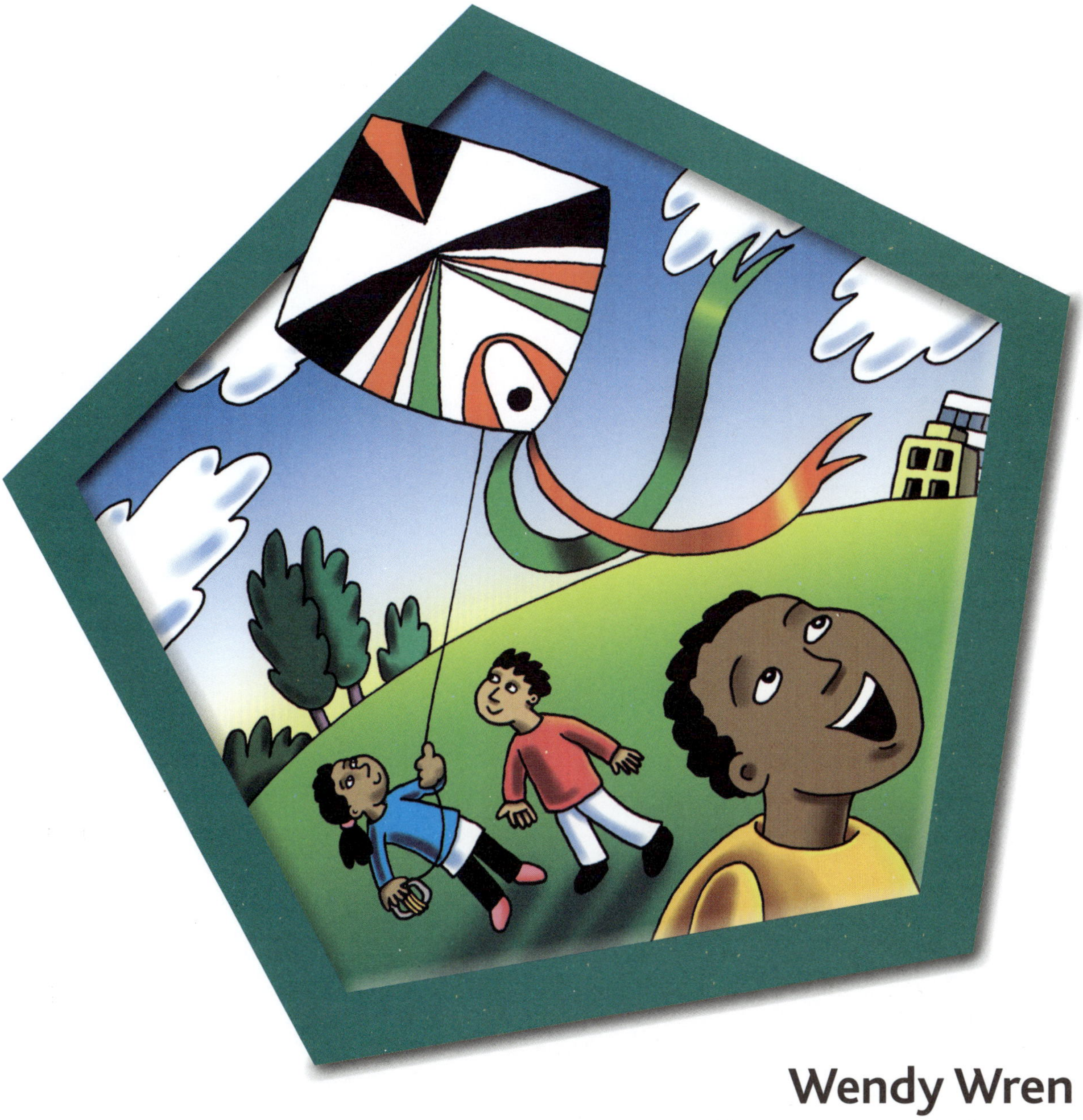

Wendy Wren
Series Editor: John Jackman

Text © Wendy Wren 2011

Original illustrations © Nelson Thornes Ltd 2011

The right of Wendy Wren to be identified as the author of this work has been asserted by them in accordance with the Copyright, Designs and Patents Act 1988.

All rights reserved. No part of this publication may be reproduced or transmitted in any form or by any means, electronic or mechanical, including photocopy, recording or any information storage and retrieval system, without permission in writing from the publisher or under licence from the Copyright Licensing Agency Limited, of Saffron House, 6–10 Kirby Street, London, EC1N 8TS.

Any person who commits any unauthorised act in relation to this publication may be liable to criminal prosecution and civil claims for damages.

Published in 2011 by:
Nelson Thornes Ltd
Delta Place
27 Bath Road
CHELTENHAM
GL53 7TH
United Kingdom

11 12 13 14 15 / 10 9 8 7 6 5 4 3 2 1

A catalogue for this book is available from the British Library

ISBN 978 1 4085 0857 2

Illustrations by Andrew Peters, Alan Rogers and Nigel Kitching

Page make-up by The OKS Group

Printed by Multivista Global Ltd

Contents

Unit 1	Nouns	4
Unit 2	Adjectives	6
Unit 3	Singular and plural	8
Unit 4	Prepositions	10
Unit 5	Sentences	12
Unit 6	Pronouns	14
Unit 7	Sentences	16
Unit 8	Nouns	18
Check-up 1	Units 1–8	20
Unit 9	Singular and plural	22
Unit 10	Adjectives	24
Unit 11	Verbs	26
Unit 12	Nouns	28
Unit 13	Sentences	30
Unit 14	Verbs	32
Unit 15	Singular and plural	34
Unit 16	Singular and plural	36
Check-up 2	Units 9–16	38
Unit 17	Nouns	40
Unit 18	Adverbs	42
Unit 19	Contractions	44
Unit 20	Nouns	46
Unit 21	Adjectives	48
Unit 22	Sentences	50
Unit 23	Sentences	52
Unit 24	Verbs	54
Unit 25	Sentences	56
Unit 26	Nouns	58
Check-up 3	Units 17–26	60

Unit 1 Nouns

Proper nouns have capital letters.

Paul   **A**ustralia   **F**ebruary

We use capital letters for titles that go with the names of people.

Mrs Hussain

Doctor Evans

Major Lewis

We use capital letters for important words in the titles of books, films and plays.

James and the **G**iant **P**each   **S**tar **W**ars

TIP
Little words such as 'a', 'an', 'the', 'and', 'but', 'in', 'on' don't usually need capital letters.

Focus

A Say your answers to these questions.

1. What is the month of your birthday?
2. What is the name of your doctor?
3. What is the title of your favourite book?
4. What is the title of your favourite film?

B Write these **proper nouns** correctly in your book.

1. lord green
2. mrs kelly
3. miss jones
4. sir ben grey
5. queen elizabeth
6. prince john
7. doctor crisp
8. lady mary smith

Practice

A Write these titles, putting in the capital letters.

1. alice in wonderland — a book
2. the secret garden — a book
3. toy story — a film
4. the wind in the willows — a book
5. spiderman — a film

B Make a list of three of your favourite books and three of your favourite films.

> **TIP**
> The first word of any title always has a capital letter.

Extension

Copy this story.
Put in the **capital letters**.

> **TIP**
> You need capital letters for:
> - the beginning of sentences
> - proper nouns
> - the pronoun 'I'.

jim had finished reading a book called the owl who was afraid of the dark. he went to the library to get a new book. he met his friend, lee. "have you read midnight adventure?" asked lee.
"yes, it is a great book," said jim.
"it was written by peter park," said lee.
"he also wrote treasure hunt. have you read that?"
"no, but i'd like to read it. i'll ask mrs brown if it is in the library," said jim. mrs brown wasn't at her desk but mr jones helped the boys to find the book.

Unit 2 Adjectives

Adjectives are describing words.
They tell us more about a person, place or thing.

 a **happy** child
 a **vast** desert
 a **muddy** boot

Numbers can be adjectives.

Number adjectives describe the number of nouns.

Number order adjectives describe the order of nouns.

three chairs   **four** books   the **first** prize   the **second** trumpet

Number order adjectives to ten are:
first, second, third, fourth, fifth, sixth, seventh, eighth, ninth, tenth.

Focus

A Say the **number order adjective** for each number.

1. five
2. three
3. nine
4. six
5. one
6. four
7. ten
8. two
9. seven
10. eight

B Match the **number adjectives** in the box on the left with the number order adjectives in the box on the right.
Write the pairs in your book.

| ninety-nine three twenty | fourteenth eighth sixth |
| fourteen six eight | twentieth third ninety-ninth |

Practice

A Copy the sentences below. Underline the **number adjectives**. Put a ring around the **nouns** they describe.

1. There are four glasses on the table.
2. We saw two seagulls on the sand.
3. I got ten answers right.
4. My coat has six pockets.
5. We need two eggs and one lemon to make the pancakes.

B Copy the sentences below. Underline the **number order adjectives**. Put a ring around the nouns they describe.

1. The sixteenth day of June is Monday.
2. The fourth book on the shelf is blue.
3. The old woman is in her eightieth year.
4. That's the third time I've told you.
5. The fifth boat in the race sank.

Extension

Look at the picture.
Copy and complete the sentences using **number order adjectives**.

Six children were in the running race. Ned was the _____ to cross the line but Claire was a close _____. Dave came in _____ and Bob was _____. Nora and Ian were _____ and _____ at the end of the race.

Unit 3: Singular and plural

Singular means one person or thing. **Plural** means more than one person or thing. To make a **noun** plural, we usually add 's'.

one hat   two hat**s**

To make nouns ending in 's', 'ch', 'sh' and 'x' plural, we add 'es'.

two bus**es**   three watch**es**   four bush**es**   five box**es**

When a noun ends in a **consonant** + 'y', we take off the 'y' and add 'ies'.

When a noun ends in a **vowel** + 'y', just add 's'.

one baby   two bab**ies**   one toy   two toy**s**

Focus

A Think of as many **nouns** as you can that:

1. make their plural with 's'
2. make their plural with 'es'
3. make their plural with 'ies'.

B Write the **plurals** of these words.

1. flask
2. class
3. farmer
4. spot
5. tray
6. match
7. hobby
8. story
9. flash
10. lorry
11. baby
12. day

Practice

A Write the **plurals** of these nouns.

1. lady
2. spy
3. lily
4. city

B Put each of the **plural nouns** from A into a sentence of your own.

> **TIP**
> Remember the capital letters and full stops.

C Write the **singular** of these nouns.

1. cherries
2. armies
3. bays
4. diaries

D Put each of the **singular** nouns from C into a sentence of your own.

Extension

Use a **plural noun** ending in 's', 'es' or 'ies' to fill each gap.

1. When the weather is hot, people often eat ice _____.
2. _____ let out smoke from the roofs of houses.
3. _____ are used to lock doors.
4. Small horses are called _____.
5. You use _____ to light a fire.
6. Very young children are called _____.
7. There are seven _____ in a week.
8. Some people live in very big _____.

Unit 4 Prepositions

A **preposition** is a word that links a noun or pronoun to another word in a sentence. The words in red are prepositions. They link the words in bold.

 The **tiger** is **in** the **tree**.

 The **boy** ran **after** the **ball**.

 **Sam** was cross **with** the **rabbit**.

 The **bird** took the food **from** the **table**.

Focus

A What is the opposite of each **preposition**?

1. outside
2. down
3. below
4. after
5. without
6. over
7. near
8. off

B Copy the sentences below. Underline the prepositions.

1. The rope was tied around the tree.
2. It was colder when the sun went behind the clouds.
3. It was very windy during the night.
4. The path went through the woods.
5. The duck flew across the lake.
6. The horse jumped over the fence.
7. The grass under the tree was brown and dry.
8. We put our bags near the door.

Practice

A Copy the sentences below.
Choose the correct **preposition** to finish each sentence.

1. I am sorry about/for breaking the plate.
2. Happy is the opposite to/of sad.
3. We played football for/during two hours.
4. No one knew the cause of/for the accident.
5. Is this book different of/from that one?

B Use each preposition in a sentence of your own.

1. between
2. behind
3. against
4. into
5. beside
6. towards

Extension

A **prepositional phrase** is a group of words that:
- begins with a **preposition**
- ends with a **noun** or **pronoun**
- tells us where something is or when something happens.

The team crowded **around the goalscorer**.

The prepositional phrase is 'around the goalscorer'.

Copy the sentences below.
Underline the **prepositional phrases**.

1. We flew over the ocean.
2. The show lasted for three hours.
3. I'll be there in five minutes.
4. I walked behind my brother.
5. He jumped on to the bed.
6. The cat chased after the mice.
7. The crops grow in good soil.
8. The swimmers dived into the sea.

Unit 5 Sentences

Simple sentences have a **subject** and an **object**.
Subjects and objects are **nouns** and **pronouns**.
The **boy** eats the **peach**.
↑ subject   ↑ object

The **subject** is who or what the sentence is about: **boy**
The **object** is who or what is having something done to it: **peach**

Here are some more examples.
The **girl** wears a **hat**.   The **man** rides a **horse**.
↑ subject ↑ object   ↑ subject ↑ object

> **TIP**
> **Nouns** are naming words. **Pronouns** are words that can take the place of nouns – for example, 'she'.

Focus

A Say which is the **subject** and which is the **object** in these sentences.

1. The boy kicked the ball.
2. I ate the cake.
3. We washed the plates.
4. Tom read the book.
5. The bird built a nest.
6. The farmer planted seeds.

B Copy the sentences below. Underline the subject in each sentence.

1. We are buying tickets.
2. I bought a jacket.
2. Kim baked a cake.
3. The stone cracked the window.
5. Asad cleaned his boots.
6. They learned their spellings

C Copy the sentences below. Underline the object in each sentence.

1. The nurse wore a uniform.
2. The bus crashed into a tree.
3. I closed the door.
4. The rabbit dug a hole.
5. He read the letter.
6. The man cut down the tree.

Practice

A Copy each sentence.
Finish each one by adding a **subject**.

1. .... climbed the tree.
2. .... finished our homework.
3. .... cooked a pie.
4. .... laid an egg.
5. .... swept the ground.

B Copy the sentences below. Finish each one by adding an **object**.

1. Jacob broke his ....
2. My dad mends ....
3. They threw the ....
4. Sam bought a ....

Extension

> **TIP**
> **Adjectives** are describing words.

A Make these sentences more interesting by putting an **adjective** in front of each **object**.

1. I saw a .... snake.
2. Mum bought a .... dress.
3. The wind blew down the .... tree.
4. Ben broke the .... window.
5. I found a .... coin.

B Write sentences of your own using these pairs of **subjects** and **objects**.

1. Subject: we — Object: ball
2. Subject: the children — Object: kitten
3. Subject: the rain — Object: garden
4. Subject: the crowd — Object: train

Unit 6 Pronouns

A **pronoun** can be used instead of a noun.

The **candle** is burning.
It is burning.

Ben hates cabbage.
He hates cabbage.

Here is a list of useful pronouns.

I	you	he	she	it	we	they
me	yourself	him	her	itself	us	them
myself	yourselves	himself	herself		ourselves	themselves

Focus

A What are the **pronouns** in these sentences?

1 Give it to me.
2 Where are you going?
3 She did it all herself.
4 They went to visit him.
5 She asked us if we had seen him.
6 We made them ourselves.

B Copy the sentences below. Choose pronouns from the box to use instead of the underlined words.

> them   he   they   it   she

1 The vase fell on the floor and <u>the vase</u> broke.
2 The zebras wanted a drink so <u>the zebras</u> went to the waterhole.
3 I told the children we would meet <u>the children</u> at one o'clock.
4 The headmaster came in and <u>the headmaster</u> spoke to us.
5 The girl got up early so that <u>the girl</u> was not late for school.

Practice

Use a **pronoun** from the box to finish each sentence.

1. Liz wants to paint the room ....
2. I want to go to the shops by ....
3. You almost cut .... with that knife.
4. The cat stretched .... in front of the fire.
5. The postman hurt .... when he fell off the bike.

> myself
> yourself
> himself
> herself
> itself

Extension

A Read the sentences. Change the **nouns** and **proper nouns** into **pronouns**. The first one is done for you.

1. Nita met her friends.

   <u>She</u> met <u>them</u>.

2. Roshan waited for the postwoman.

   .... waited for ....

3. Sam and I waved to Lee.

   .... waved to ....

4. Dan and Becky watched the cricket match.

   .... watched ....

B Use each of these pronouns in sentences of your own.

1. yourself
2. they
3. myself
4. her
5. us
6. ourselves

Unit 7 Sentences

Direct speech is when we write the actual words that someone has said. It can be written in speech bubbles like in this picture.

If we want to write this as a conversation, we have to use **inverted commas** at the beginning and the end of the spoken words.

When a different person speaks, we start a new line.

"Lovely fresh oranges!" shouted the woman.
"I'll have two, please," said the other woman.

TIP
Inverted commas are also called **speech marks**.

Focus

A Look at the sentences. Say the spoken words.

1. "I'm very late," said the man.
2. "This is great music," said Grace.
3. "What time is it?" asked Mum.
4. "I've lost my book," he said.

B Copy the spoken words in each sentence.

1. "I must cut the grass today," said Mum.
2. "Let me look at your arm," said the doctor.
3. "May we have an ice cream?" asked the children.

TIP
Don't forget the **inverted commas**.

C Copy the sentences below. Put **inverted commas** around the spoken words.

1. I like making people laugh, said the boy.
2. I have lost my lunchbox, said the girl.
3. I am thirsty, said Mia.
4. This window is broken, said the angry man.

TIP
Find the words that are spoken. Put " in front of them and " at the end.

Practice

A Look at this conversation. Inverted commas are used at the start and end of spoken words. A new line is started when a different person speaks.

"Did you see the rabbit go down that hole?" said the farmer.

"No," said Mary.

"Look over there by that big tree," said the farmer.

"Oh yes! The rabbit has just popped up again," said Mary.

"It might not be the same one. There are lots of rabbits down that hole," said the farmer.

B Copy the conversation below. Add inverted commas around spoken words and start a new line when a different person speaks.

How many brothers and sisters have you got? asked Jane. I have three brothers and one sister, said Ben. Are they older or younger than you? asked Jane. Two of my brothers and my sister are older, said Jane.

Extension

A Always using the word 'said' in conversations is not very interesting. What word has been used instead of 'said' in these sentences?

1. "I scored a goal!" he shouted.
2. "Be quiet!" she whispered.
3. "Where are you going?" she asked.
4. "I've hurt my leg," he cried.

B Write a **direct speech sentence** using each of these words.

1. muttered
2. yelled
3. called
4. ordered
5. mumbled
6. explained

Unit 8 Nouns

A **noun** is the name of a person, place or thing.

A **collective noun** is a special name for a group of people, places or things.

box

house

a **swarm** of bees

a **fleet** of ships

Focus

A What is the **collective noun** for each of these?

1. A group of trees.
2. A group of sheep.
3. A group of cows.
4. A group of birds.

B Choose a word from the box to go with each collective noun. Write them in your book.

> books   wolves   flowers   trees   footballers   people

1. a forest of ....
2. a crowd of ....
3. a bunch of ....
4. a team of ....
5. a pack of ....
6. a library of ....

Practice

A What would you expect to find in these groups? Use your dictionary to help you.

1. an army
2. a crew
3. a pride
4. an orchestra
5. a bouquet
6. a gaggle

B Sometimes we use the same **collective noun** for different things. Find two things for each of these collective nouns.

1. a pack of ....
   and ....

2. a herd of ....
   and ....

3. a bunch of ....
   and ....

4. a flock of ....
   and ....

Extension

A Copy the sentences below. Fill each gap with a **collective noun**.

1. The boy ran up the .... of stairs.
2. A .... of people watched the match.
3. The .... of fish swam in the sea.
4. The .... scored two goals.

B Choose five collective nouns and use them in sentences of your own.

Check-up 1

Proper nouns

A Write these names correctly.

1. mary jones
2. kamal khan
3. doctor finch

B Write these book titles correctly.

1. a tale of two cities
2. charlie and the chocolate factory

Adjectives

A Copy the sentences below. Underline the **number adjectives**.

1. Five ponies are in the field.
2. I planted twenty trees.

B Use these **number order adjectives** in sentences of your own.

1. eighth
2. fortieth
3. hundredth
4. first

Singular and plural

Write the **plurals** of these nouns.

1. berry
2. key
3. post
4. penny
5. ruby
6. kidney

Prepositions

A Copy the sentences below. Fill each gap with a **preposition**.

1. I will hide _____ the shed.
2. "It is very cold _____," said Mum.

B Use each preposition in a sentence of your own.

1. beneath   2. around   3. during   4. inside

Sentences

A Copy the sentences below. Underline the **subject** of each sentence.

1. The goat ate the grass.
2. We like to ride our bicycles.
3. The play was very funny.
4. The boys went for a long walk.

B Copy the sentences below. Underline the **object** of each sentence.

1. Jay ate an ice cream.
2. Mrs Potter cleaned the windows.
3. I like oranges.
4. I picked an apple.

C Copy the sentences below. Put **inverted commas** around the spoken words.

1. Let me clean that cut, said the nurse.
2. I've scored a goal! shouted Ethan.

Pronouns

Copy the sentences below. Underline the **pronouns**.

1. I am going to tidy the room myself.
2. He watched the bird as it dived for the fish.
3. When you go out, see if you can see it.

Collective nouns

Use the following **collective nouns** in sentences of your own.

1. herd   2. band   3. bouquet   4. crowd

Unit 9: Singular and plural

Singular means **one**. **Plural** means **more than one**.

To make a noun plural, we usually add 's'.

tree – tree**s**
rabbit – rabbit**s**

To make nouns ending in 's', 'ch', 'sh' and 'x' plural, add 'es'.

glass – glass**es**   bush – bush**es**
match – match**es**   box – box**es**

When a noun ends in a **consonant** + 'y', take off the 'y' and add 'ies'.

baby – bab**ies**
lorry – lorr**ies**

When a noun ends in a **vowel** + 'y', just add 's'.

chimney – chimney**s**
toy – toy**s**

Nouns ending in 'f' and 'fe' are made plural by changing the 'f' or 'fe' to 'v' and adding 'es'.

  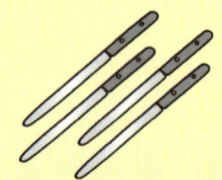

wolf – wol**ves**   shelf – shel**ves**   knife – kni**ves**

Focus

A Say the **plurals** of these **nouns**.

1. farmer
2. watch
3. pony
4. book
5. fox
6. day
7. lady
8. flash

B Write the plurals of these nouns.

1. calf
2. knife
3. life
4. sheaf

Practice

A Write the **plurals** of these nouns. Put them in a sentence of your own.

1. leaf
2. loaf
3. shelf
4. scarf

B Write the **singular** of these nouns. Put them in a sentence of your own.

1. hooves
2. wolves
3. halves
4. thieves

Extension

For some 'f' and 'fe' words just add 's'.
There is no rule. You just have to learn them!

chief	chief**s**	cliff	cliff**s**	belief	belief**s**
gulf	gulf**s**	sheriff	sheriff**s**	oaf	oaf**s**
reef	reef**s**	roof	roof**s**	handkerchief	handkerchief**s**

A Use a **plural** noun ending in 'ves' or 's' to finish each sentence.

1. People who steal things are called ....
2. We use .... for blowing our noses.
3. .... are used for cutting.
4. .... grow on trees.
5. Horses have four ....
6. .... kept law and order in America's Wild West.

B Write three nouns that make their plural:

1. by adding 's'
2. by adding 'es'
3. by adding 'ies'
4. by adding 'ves'.

Unit 10 Adjectives

Adjectives are words that describe nouns.
a **long** snake   a **cold** day   a **small** tree

We use a **comparative adjective** to compare **two** things.
This rope is **longer** than that rope.

We use a **superlative adjective** to compare **three or more** things.
This rope is the **longest** of the three.

For adjectives that end in 'y', change the 'y' to 'i' and add 'er' or 'est'.

Adjective	Comparative	Superlative
wind**y**	wind**ier**	wind**iest**

If the adjective is a long word and does not end in 'y':
- we put the word 'more' in front of it to compare two things
- we put the word 'most' in front of it to compare three or more things.

Adjective	Comparative	Superlative
beautiful	**more** beautiful	**most** beautiful

Focus

A Which would you say?

1. enormouser or more enormous?
2. most intelligent or intelligentest?
3. famousest or most famous?

B Copy the table. Fill in the missing **adjectives**.

Adjective	Comparative	Superlative
round	----------	roundest
----------	shorter	----------
----------	----------	heaviest
terrible	----------	----------

Practice

A Copy the sentences below.
Make the adjectives in the brackets into **comparative adjectives**.

1. That question is (easy) than the last one.
2. It is (cloudy) than yesterday.
3. Our cat is (intelligent) than our rabbit.
4. This plum is (juicy) than that one.

B Copy the sentences below.
Make the adjectives in the brackets into **superlative adjectives**.

1. This is the (smelly) of all the cheeses.
2. He is the (lazy) boy in school.
3. This is the (peaceful) place I have ever been.
4. She is the (important) person in our town.

Extension

A Use the **comparative** or **superlative** of an adjective from the box to compare each set of things. The first one is done for you.

1. Compare the weight of two loaves.
   The white loaf is heavy. The brown loaf is heavier.
2. Compare the surface of two roads.
3. Compare the weather on three days.
4. Compare the age of three fossils.
5. Compare the neatness of two rooms.

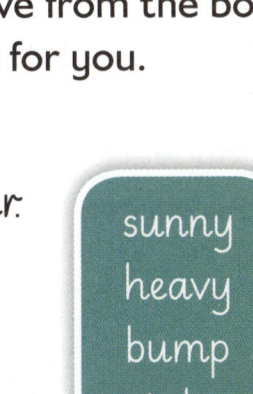

sunny
heavy
bump
tidy
old

B Use these comparative and superlative adjectives in sentences of your own.

1. messier   2. more nervous   3. cheekiest   4. most dangerous

Unit 11 Verbs

When we write about what has happened in the past, we use **past tense verbs**.
To make the **simple past tense**, we usually add 'ed' or 'd' to the verb family name.

I comb**ed** my hair.   I wash**ed** my face.   I clos**ed** the door.

The **past continuous tense** is very useful.
We use it when an action goes on for some time or when something else happens at the same time.

I **was walking** when it started to rain.
We **were playing** football for three hours.
He **was reading** when the telephone rang.

We make the past continuous tense like this:

Simple past tense of 'to be'	+ verb family name	+ ing	Past continous tense
I was	sing	ing	I was singing
you were	point	ing	you were pointing
he/she/it was	listen	ing	he/she/it was listening
we were	jump	ing	we were jumping
you were	shout	ing	you were shouting
they were	talk	ing	they were talking

Focus

A Say these verbs in the **simple past tense** and then in the **past continuous tense**.

1. smile
2. find
3. brush
4. catch
5. sleep
6. grow
7. dig
8. clean

B Copy the sentences below. Underline the past continuous tense in each one.

1. The birds were flying around the garden.
2. The tree was bending in the wind.
3. The boy was playing in the leaves.

Practice

Copy the sentences below.
Use the **past continuous tense** instead of the verb family name given in the brackets.

> **TIP**
> Use the past tense of the verb 'to be' and an 'ing' word.

1. Jill (to post) a letter when she saw her friend.
2. The children (to talk) until the teacher came in.
3. I (to hope) to cut the grass but it started to rain.

Extension

A Copy this table and fill in the missing **verbs**.

Verb family name	Simple past tense ('ed' or 'd')	Past continuous tense ('to be' + 'ing')
to save	_____	we _____
to follow	_____	it _____
to bake	_____	they _____
_____	smiled	you _____
to carry	_____	I _____

B Copy the sentences below.
Fill in the gaps with **past continuous** verbs.

1. I _____ when it began to snow.
2. We _____ when we saw an accident.

Unit 12 Nouns

Possessive nouns tell you who owns something.
They have an **apostrophe** and an 's' at the end.
Ruth**'s** bicycle
Ruth is the owner.

Ruth's bicycle means **the bicycle belonging to Ruth**.
Ruth's is the possessive noun.
Roger**'s** book.
Roger is the owner.

Roger's book means **the book belonging to Roger**.
Roger's is the possessive noun.
The **'s** tells you who or what is the owner.

Focus

A Say who the owner is.

1. Sam's hat
2. the girl's book
3. Fred's homework
4. the horse's tail
5. the team's name
6. Kim's question

B Copy these into your book.
Underline the owner in each one.

1. Tim's football
2. the girl's laugh
3. the flower's stem
4. the doctor's coat
5. the cat's collar
6. the car's engine
7. John's shoe
8. the farmer's field
9. the captain's ship
10. the boy's hair

Practice

TIP: The apostrophe comes before the 's'.

Copy the sentences below.
Add an **apostrophe** to the owner in each sentence.

1. Jims homework was very hard.
2. He found the girls toy in the park.
3. That mans tie is blue with red spots.
4. The cats claws are very sharp.
5. The flowers petals have fallen off.
6. The books cover was torn.
7. The boys pen was in his pocket.
8. Ninas wish came true.
9. I like Amys coat.
10. I found the old womans scarf.

Extension

A Write these in a shorter way, using **possessive nouns**.

1. the hand belonging to the girl
2. the dinner belonging to the boy
3. the tail belonging to the mouse
4. the song belonging to the bird
5. the wheels belonging to the car

B Use these possessive nouns in sentences of your own.

1. the bird's wing
2. the shop's window
3. the horse's hooves
4. the man's voice
5. the lady's umbrella
6. the tiger's tail

Unit 13 Sentences

TIP
Remember that a sentence needs a capital letter and a full stop or question mark.

A sentence has two parts.

The **subject** is the person or thing the sentence is about.
The **predicate** is the rest of the sentence.

Subject	Predicate
The eagle	is a large bird.
My bucket	has a hole in it.

Subject	Predicate
Rabbits	live in burrows.
I	have a kitten.

Focus

A What is the **subject** of each sentence?

1. The coat was dirty.
2. My bicycle is broken.
3. Tom is unhappy.
4. The garden was neat and tidy.
5. This house is very old.
6. He likes eating apples.

B Copy the sentences below.
Underline the subject in each sentence.

1. I have hurt my knee.
2. Sharks live in the sea.
3. The doctor is very busy.
4. The horses are in the field.
5. My rabbit is very old.

C Copy the sentences below.
Underline the **predicate** in each sentence.

1. The shop opens at nine o'clock.
2. We went to the park.
3. Dad is a very good cook.

Practice

Match each **subject** with a **predicate** to make a sensible sentence. The first one is done for you.

The cottage — watched the match.
I — was very exciting.
The race — was near the river.
A big crowd — wrote the answers.
Sam — am eating my lunch.

Extension

A Write an interesting **subject** for each of these **predicates**.

1. .... fell into the pond.
2. .... were afraid of the dark.
3. .... saw my brother score a goal.
4. .... left her bag on the bus.
5. .... was cold and wet.
6. .... grew very tall.

B Write an interesting predicate for each of these subjects.

1. The apple ....
2. The big forest ....
3. They ....
4. Some birds ....
5. The old man ....
6. This book ....

Unit 14 Verbs

Verbs tell us what action is happening. The **tense** of a verb tells us when an action happened.

If the action is happening in the present, we use a **present tense verb**.
If the action happened in the past, we use a **past tense verb**.
If we are writing about what is going to happen in the future, we use a **future tense verb**.

She **knits** a jumper.　　　She **is knitting** a jumper.
He **climbed** the mountain.　　He **was climbing** the mountain.
I **shall hold** the ladder.　　He **will save** the cat.

The **future tense** is made up of two parts:
- the word 'shall' after the pronouns 'I' and 'we', and the word 'will' after the pronouns 'you', 'he', 'she', 'it' and 'they'
- the **verb family name**.

Focus

A Are the following written in the **present**, **past** or **future tense**?

1. I am singing.
2. He will read.
3. I was walking.
4. We shall talk.
5. She slept.
6. You laugh.

B Copy the sentences below.
Underline the **future tense verbs**.

1. We shall take an umbrella with us.
2. He will wrap the present this afternoon.
3. The children will know when to sing.
4. I shall play football on Saturday.
5. It will be sunny tomorrow.

Practice

A Copy the sentences below.
Change the **present tense verbs** to **future tense verbs**.

1. Kim answers the questions.
2. We are walking to school.
3. The farmer plants his seeds.
4. I read my book.

B Copy the sentences below. Change the **past tense verbs** to future tense verbs.

1. Fred walked along the beach.
2. The cars raced around the track.
3. We bought some new pencils.

C Copy the table. Fill in the missing **verbs**.

Verb family	Present tense	Past tense	Future tense
to give	I am _____	I _____	I shall give
to _____	they speak	they _____	they _____ _____
to work	she is _____	she was _____	she _____ _____
to _____	we look	we were _____	we _____ _____

Extension

If we want to make a strong statement, we can:
• put 'will' after 'I' and 'we'
• put 'shall' after 'you', 'he', 'she', 'it' and 'they'.

Copy the sentences below. Put 'shall' or 'will' in each gap to make a strong statement.

1. You _____ go to bed at nine o'clock!
2. I _____ ride my bike down the lane.
3. He _____ not go to the park!

Unit 15: Singular and plural

Nouns can be **singular** or **plural**. **Verbs** can also be singular or plural.

When we use a **singular noun**, we must also use a **singular verb**.
The **house needs** painting.

singular noun   singular verb

When we use a **plural noun**, we must use a **plural verb**.
The **houses need** painting.

plural noun   plural verb

The verb families 'to be' and 'to have' can be tricky. You must learn them.

Verb family	Simple present tense		Simple past tense	
	singular	plural	singular	plural
to be	I am you are he/she/it is	we are you are they are	I was you were he/she/it was	we were you were they were
to have	I have you have he/she/it has	we have you have they have	I had you had he/she/it had	we had you had they had

Focus

A Which would you say?

1. The parrots squawks.   or   The parrots squawk.
2. You have won.   or   You has won.
3. We was playing.   or   We were playing.
4. The boy kick the ball.   or   The boy kicks the ball.

B Copy the sentences below. Choose the correct **verb** to finish each one.

1. The houses is/are empty.
2. We is/are going to buy them.
3. I is/am going to live in one of them.

Practice

Some of these are collective nouns. They are followed by a singular verb, for example: The army marches quickly.

A Put each of these **nouns** into a sentence, followed by 'has' or 'have'.

1. crowd
2. children
3. team
4. girls
5. everyone
6. mice
7. oxen
8. herd

B Copy the sentences below. Choose the correct **verb** to finish each one.

1. The cake crumble/crumbles when you cut it.
2. The icing is/are very soft.
3. We buy/buys a cake every week.
4. My sisters like/likes lemon cake.

Extension

TIP
You are looking for **eight** mistakes.

Copy this passage. Correct the mistakes.

We goes to the library on a Saturday morning. I likes to read adventure stories but my sister like books about animals. We takes three books home every week. The man in the library are very helpful. If he haven't got the book I wants, he order it for me.

Unit 16 Singular and plural

Singular nouns are made **plural** in different ways.

	Singular	Plural
For most nouns, add 's'.	jacket	jacket**s**
For nouns ending in 's', 'ch', 'sh' and 'x', add 'es'.	class	class**es**
For nouns ending in a **consonant** + 'y', take off the 'y' and add 'ies'.	family	famil**ies**
For nouns ending in a **vowel** + 'y', just add 's'.	trolley	trolley**s**
For nouns ending in 'o', we usually add 'es'.	tomato	tomato**es**
For musical nouns ending in 'o', and for nouns ending in 'oo', just add 's'.	piano bamboo	piano**s** bamboo**s**

Some nouns do not follow any of these rules. They have a plural that is a different word, for example:

Singular	Plural
child	children
goose	geese
person	people

Focus

TIP Use a dictionary for words you do not know.

A What would you say?

1. one woman but two _____
2. one tooth but three _____
3. one foot but two _____
4. one mouse but six _____

B Make these singular nouns **plural**.

1. photo
2. cello
3. potato
4. hippo
5. hero
6. volcano
7. echo
8. piccolo

C Make these singular nouns plural.

1 woman 2 tooth 3 ox 4 foot 5 postman

Practice

A Copy the sentences below. Write 'is' or 'are' in the gaps.

1 The piano .... being mended.
2 The mice .... chewing the rope.
3 The hippos .... playing in the mud.
4 The postwoman .... carrying letters.

B Copy the sentences below. Write 'was' or 'were' in the gaps.

1 The children .... having tea.
2 This man .... a farmer.
3 The cockatoos .... colourful birds.
4 The tomato .... ripe.

Extension

A Use a dictionary to find the **plural** of these nouns.

1 cod 2 mackerel 3 salmon 4 sheep 5 deer

B Some words are always plural. Write the names of the pictures in your book.

1  2  3  4

Check-up 2

Singular and plural

Write the **plurals** of these nouns.

1. calf
2. life
3. loaf
4. gulf
5. dwarf
6. knife
7. thief
8. cliff
9. goose
10. piano
11. mouse
12. deer

Adjectives

A Write the **comparative** of each adjective.

1. calm
2. important
3. loud
4. sleepy
5. funny
6. marvellous
7. white
8. bumpy

B Write the **superlative** of each adjective.

1. happy
2. enjoyable
3. hard
4. old
5. dirty
6. dangerous
7. muddy
8. lonely

Verbs

Copy the sentences below. Underline the **past tense verb** in each one.

1. The children were laughing all the time.
2. We quickly walked up the hill.
3. Ben hurried to the shops.
4. The pig was rolling in the mud.
5. I was working hard all day.

Nouns

A Copy the sentences below. Underline the **owner** in each sentence.
1. Mary's umbrella is yellow.
2. The man's car is broken.
3. The giraffe's neck is long.
4. The tiger's feet are huge.

B Copy the sentences below. Add an **apostrophe** to the owner.
1. The childs face was dirty.
2. The cats teeth are sharp.
3. The kittens fur is soft.
4. Rons bicycle is in the shed.

C Write these in a shorter way, using **possessive nouns**.
1. the birthday present belonging to Bill
2. the car belonging to Mum
3. the tail belonging to the rat

Sentences

A Copy the sentences below. Underline the **subject** in each sentence.
1. I catch a bus to school every day.
2. Swallows fly south for the winter.

B Finish these sentences with interesting **predicates**.
1. The old ship _____
2. My younger brother _____

Singular and plural

Copy and correct these sentences.
1. Dad and I is going for a walk.
2. Everyone have gone out.
3. My sister were in the choir.
4. The mice lives in the barn.

Unit 17 Nouns

TIP
Nouns are naming words.

There are many different types of nouns.

Common nouns tell us the names of ordinary things.

monkey

table

Proper nouns tell us the names of special things.

Mr Parvez

India

Collective nouns tell us the names of groups of things.

a **flock** of sheep

Compound nouns are made by joining two nouns together.

rain + bow = **rainbow**

Focus

A Say what type of **noun** each of these are.

1. boy
2. River Thames
3. library
4. Joe
5. window
6. lion
7. herd
8. April
9. team

B Write the **compound noun** for each of these pictures.

1.
2.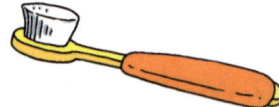
3.

Practice

Choose a **noun** from the box on the left and another from the box on the right and put them together to make a **compound noun**.

space
neck
tea
door
rain
book

lace
ship
cup
coat
mark
step

Extension

 **A** Make a list of the **compound nouns** you can find in this story.

It was the day of the important football match. Jack was excited because he was the team goalkeeper. He was so excited he forgot to do his homework! His schoolteacher was not very pleased! At twelve o'clock, the team went out. They walked along the footpath to get to the pitch. Jack put his tracksuit by the sideline and waited for the match to begin.

 B Use these compound nouns in sentences of your own.

1. flowerbed
2. hillside
3. daylight
4. housework
5. waterfall
6. stairway

Unit 18 Adverbs

An **adverb** tells us more about how, when or where the action of a verb takes place.

How?	Bill clapped **loudly**.
When?	Mary fell off her bike **yesterday**.
Where?	I put the flowers **outside**.

Some adverbs tell us more about other adverbs.
I walked **very quickly**.   It rained **quite heavily**.

We can use **comparative** and **superlative adverbs** to compare actions just as we use adjectives to compare nouns.

Comparative adverbs compare two actions.
Superlative adverbs compare three or more actions.

For adverbs ending in 'ly', add 'more' and 'most'.

Adverb	Comparative	Superlative
clearly	**more** clearly	**most** clearly
friendly	**more** friendly	**most** friendly

For adverbs that do not end in 'ly', add 'er' and 'est'.

Adverb	Comparative	Superlative
hard	hard**er**	hard**est**
high	high**er**	high**est**

Some adverbs do not follow any rules. You just have to learn them.

Adverb	Comparative	Superlative
well	better	best
badly	worse	worst

Focus

A Say if the adverb is telling you how, when or where.

1 inside   2 earlier   3 slowly   4 today   5 here

B Write the **comparative** and **superlative** of these adverbs.

1 easily   2 happily   3 badly   4 widely   5 late

Practice

A Change the adverbs in brackets into **comparative** adverbs.

1 We use the sledge (often) when it snows for a long time.
2 The vegetables grew (well) after we watered them.
3 "You must try (hard)," said the teacher.
4 I wrote (neatly) in my book with my new pen.

B Change the adverbs in brackets into **superlative** adverbs.

1 Ben tried (hard) and won the race.
2 You have scored (badly) in the test.
3 I did my homework (carefully).
4 I jumped (high) in my class.

Extension

> **TIP**
> The **second** word in the brackets gives you a clue to the adverb you need.

A Replace the words in brackets with one **adverb**.

1 The nurse helped the hurt boy (with calmness).
2 Ali kicked the ball (with skill).
3 He shouted at the boy (with anger).
4 I walked along (with quietness).

B Use these **comparative** and **superlative** adverbs in sentences of your own.

1 worse
2 more honestly
3 widest
4 most clearly
5 more sensibly
6 earliest

Unit 19 Contractions

Contractions are words that have been made smaller by missing out a letter or letters.

I am = **I'm**   you are = **you're**

We put an **apostrophe** in place of the missing letter or letters.

"**That's** not right," said John. "A square **doesn't** have five corners."

That's = that is   **doesn't** = does not

Focus

A Say what the **contraction** of each word is.

1. cannot
2. will not
3. does not
4. I am
5. he is
6. they are
7. have not
8. we will

B Write these contractions in full.

1. who's
2. they'll
3. he's
4. you're
5. doesn't
6. there's
7. who'd
8. shouldn't
9. we've

C Write the contractions for these pairs of words.

1. would not
2. have not
3. she has
4. we are
5. we shall
6. has not
7. who would
8. will not
9. let us

Practice

Copy the conversation below. Change the underlined words into **contractions**.

"I <u>cannot</u> find my hat anywhere!" shouted Ben. "<u>I have</u> seen it in my room but <u>it is</u> not there now!"

"If <u>you would</u> put things away, <u>you would</u> be able to find them," said his mother. "<u>I shall</u> come and help you when <u>I have</u> finished writing this letter."

"<u>I shall</u> ask Sam," said Ben. "<u>He will</u> know where it is. I think <u>he has</u> got it!"

Extension

A Write the **contraction** from each sentence. Next to it, write the words it replaces.

1. "The ball's gone into the pond," shouted Pam.
2. "We'll need a long stick to get it out," said Dad.
3. "I'll go and look in the shed," said Pam.
4. "There's one by the door," said Dad.
5. "I'll be back in a minute," said Pam.

B Write a conversation between two people. Use as many of the contractions from the box as you can.

TIP
Remember to use **speech marks**.

can't   he'll   she's   haven't   it's   they've   won't   don't

Unit 20 Nouns

A **possessive noun** tells us who owns something. Where there is one owner, we add **'s** to the noun.

 the tiger**'s** roar

 the baby**'s** rattle

TIP
If there is one owner, the noun is **singular**. If there is more than one owner, the noun is **plural**.

Where there is more than one owner:
- we add **'** if there is already an 's' at the end of the word
- we add **'s** if there is not an 's' at the end of the word.

 the boys**'** sledges

 the cats**'** tails

 the children**'s** hats

 the oxen**'s** tails

Focus

A Say if these have one owner or more than one owner?

1. the girl's gloves
2. the cats' bowl
3. the people's town
4. the men's football
5. the birds' nest
6. the lion's mane

B Add the apostrophes to show the owners. All the owners are **singular**.

1. the sheds roof
2. the girls idea
3. the rabbits hutch
4. the clocks hands
5. Jans bicycle
6. the mans scarf
7. Toms face
8. the teapots lid
9. the buckets handle

Practice

Change these by using **possessive nouns**.
All the owners are **plural**. The first one is done for you.

1. the cave of the thieves
   the thieves' cave
2. the meeting of the parents
3. the homework of the children
4. the headlines of the newspapers
5. the race of the men
6. the mothers of the girls
7. the trunks of the trees
8. the belts of the coats

Extension

A Copy the sentences below.
Is the owner in each one **singular** or **plural**?
Add the apostrophe to the owner or owners.

1. The twins birthday is in January.
2. The policemans helmet fell on the ground.
3. The boys school uniforms are blue.
4. Mr Browns house is next to the bus stop.
5. The mountains top is covered in clouds.
6. My three sisters bedroom is always messy.

B Use these **plural possessive nouns** in sentences of your own.

1. ships'
2. cousins'
3. women's
4. friends'
5. windows'
6. farmers'
7. teams'
8. tigers'
9. fields'

47

Unit 21 Adjectives

Adjectives describe and compare nouns.
We can describe a jumper using an adjective.
a **dirty** jumper

We can compare two jumpers using a **comparative adjective**.
a **dirty** jumper   a **dirtier** jumper

We can compare three or more jumpers using a **superlative adjective**.
a **dirty** jumper   a **dirtier** jumper   the **dirtiest** jumper

Some adjectives change completely in their comparative and superlative forms. You have to learn them.

Adjective	Comparative	Superlative
bad	worse	worst
good	better	best
little	less	least
much	many	more
many	more	most
some	more	most

Focus

A Say what the **comparative** and the **superlative** of each **adjective** is.

1. short
2. frightening
3. tall
4. sad
5. cold
6. beautiful
7. warm
8. happy

B Copy the sentences below.
Choose the correct adjective to fill each gap.

1. This is the better/best party I have ever had.
2. That is the scares/scariest spider have ever seen.
3. Today was the worse/worst day of the week.
4. Do you like this book less/least than that one?

Practice

Copy the table and fill in the missing **adjectives**.

Adjective	Comparative	Superlative
silly	....	silliest
good	....	....
marvellous	....	most marvellous
....	less	....
....	....	happiest
wonderful	....	....
some	....	....
....	....	worst
....	more comfortable	....
new	....	....
long	....	....
....	....	windiest

Extension

Write sentences using these **adjectives**.

1. The comparative of important
2. The superlative of good
3. The superlative of frightening
4. The comparative of small
5. The comparative of some
6. The superlative of bad
7. The superlative of sleepy
8. The comparative of heavy
9. The superlative of terrible
10. The comparative of wise

Unit 22 Sentences

Sentences have two parts.
The **subject** tells you who or what the sentence is about.
The **predicate** is the rest of the sentence.

The cottage was in the wood.
↑   ↑
subject   **predicate**

This is a simple sentence. It does not tell us very much.

We can make the sentence more interesting by:
- adding to the subject

The **old, deserted** cottage was in the wood.
- adding to the predicate

The **old, deserted** cottage was in the **dark, gloomy** wood.

TIP
We have added **adjectives** to the sentence.

Focus

A What is the **subject** of each sentence?

1. The farmer lived in a cottage.
2. My sister has a horse.
3. The children are working hard.
4. I like singing.
5. The tree has died.
6. They are going home.

B Copy the sentences below. Underline the subject in blue. Underline the **predicate** in red.

1. The pillow was on the bed.
2. The giraffe is drinking.
3. I like to read my book.
4. Al is cooking dinner.
5. The girls are playing football.
6. My bicycle is very dirty.
7. The fire is burning brightly.
8. The shop is closed.

Practice

TIP: Use **adjectives** to make the **subject** more interesting.

A Copy the sentences below. Underline the **subject**. Write each sentence again, making the subject more interesting.

1. The butterfly sat on the leaf.
2. Monkeys live in the jungle.
3. A package came this morning.
4. The boy hid behind a tree.
5. The lion was in a cage.

B Copy the sentences below. Underline the **predicate**. Write each sentence again, making the predicate more interesting.

TIP: Use **adjectives** to make the **predicate** more interesting.

1. I went to the shop.
2. John has a bicycle.
3. I have lost my book.
4. The house is on the hill.
5. The girl played with her toy.

Extension

'I' is used as the subject of a sentence: **I** saw a cat in the old house. 'Me' is used in the predicate of a sentence: Mum is taking **me** to the football match.

Copy the sentences below. Fill each gap with 'I' or 'me'.

1. _____ am cooking meat for dinner.
2. Will you get _____ a drink?
3. Katy and _____ are going swimming.
4. The story frightened Stephen and _____.

Unit 23 Sentences

Direct speech is when we write the words someone says. We use **inverted commas** to show the words that are spoken.

"I feel cold**,"** said Nick.

We begin a new line when a different person speaks.

"I feel cold," said Nick.

"So do I," said Kim.

After the spoken words, we need some **punctuation**.
Usually, we use a **comma**.   "I feel cold**,**" said Tom.
We can also use a **question mark**.   "Do you feel cold**?**" asked Mum.
We can also use an **exclamation mark**. "I'm frozen**!**" shouted Tom.

The punctuation after the spoken words always comes before the inverted commas.

> **TIP**
> Inverted commas are also called **speech marks**.

Focus

A Should these have a **question mark** or an **exclamation mark**?

1. "Where are you going"
2. "Look out"
3. "Help me"
4. "Who are you"
5. "Oh dear"
6. "Are you lost"

B Copy the sentences below. Put **inverted commas** around the spoken words.

1. Mum is coming, said Ann.
2. What's the time? asked Nina.
3. Watch out! shouted the farmer.
4. I'm bored, said John.
5. What's the matter? asked Dad.

Practice

Copy the sentences below. Put in all the missing punctuation. Each sentence needs:
- inverted commas
- a question mark or an exclamation mark after the spoken words
- a full stop at the end.

1. Grab the rope shouted the climber
2. May I have an apple asked Mary
3. I have lost my money sobbed Tamim
4. Have you got a ticket asked the bus driver
5. What a beautiful sunset said Mum

Extension

Sometimes the words that tell us who is speaking come before the spoken words.

Dad said, "You can watch the television after tea."

When this happens, we always use a **comma**.

The boy mumbled, "I don't know the answer."

The teacher said, "Please learn it for tomorrow."

Copy the sentences below. Put in the missing punctuation.

1. Where is the treasure asked the pirate
2. Jim said I have got a map
3. Let me see it said the pirate
4. Jim asked Can I come with you to find the treasure
5. No said the pirate
6. That's not fair shouted Jim

Unit 24 Verbs

Verbs tell us what is happening. The **verb tense** tells us when it is happening.

Present tense

We make the **simple present tense** by using the **verb family name**.
I **walk** to school.   He **writes** a letter.

We make the **present continuous tense** by using the verb 'to be' and an 'ing' word.
We **are singing**.   The boys **are playing**.

Past tense

We make the **simple past tense** by adding 'd' or 'ed' to the verb family name.
The old woman **smiled**.   Sally **talked** to her friend.
Some verbs do not follow the rule, for example: tell – told, write – wrote.

We make the **past continuous tense** by using the verb 'to be' and an 'ing' word.
The old woman **was smiling**.   Sally **was talking** to her friend.

Future tense

We make the **future tense** by using the verb 'to be' and the **verb family name**.
I **shall go** at seven o'clock.   They **will meet** me.

Focus

Copy the table. Fill in the missing **verbs**.

Verb family	Present tense	Past tense	Future tense
to walk	I walk	I walked	I shall walk
	I am walking	I was walking	
to bring	you ___	you ___	you ___
	you ___	you ___	
to find	we ___	we ___	we ___
	we ___	we ___	

Practice

Copy the sentences below.
After each sentence write whether it is **present**, **past**, or **future tense**.

1. I am sewing seven buttons on my jacket.
2. The school children wore bright red uniforms.
3. I shall pack my bag in the morning.
4. She was making a cake when the doorbell rang.
5. The bird pecked at the ground.

Extension

A Write these sentences in the **past tense**.

1. My neighbour is working in the garden.
2. This plant pot is broken.
3. The lion is frightening the people.
4. The rabbit eats the carrot.
5. I go to the shops every morning.

B Write these sentences in the **future tense**.

1. The bell rang at midnight.
2. It happens every day at four o'clock.
3. I ate my tea very quickly.
4. The cat washes her new kittens.

C Use these **tenses** in sentences of your own.

1. am looking
2. were watching
3. shall go
4. eats
5. will buy
6. was sleeping

Unit 25 Sentences

Contractions that end in 'n't' and the words 'no', 'not', 'nothing', 'never' and 'nowhere' are negative words.

By using these words, we change the meaning of a sentence.

 He has an ice cream. This is a **positive** sentence.

 He **doesn't** have an ice cream. This is a **negative** sentence.

We do not use two negative words in one sentence.

I do **not** have **no** money.

This means that you do have some money!

The correct sentence is: I do **not** have **any** money.

Focus

A Say whether the following are **positive** or **negative**.

1. no books
2. some apples
3. nothing happens
4. never again
5. don't like
6. have some

B Add a **negative word** to each sentence to make it mean the opposite.

1. I .... have an apple for lunch.
2. She has .... time to tidy her room.
3. There is .... room in the cupboard.
4. We .... like walking in the rain.
5. I .... lift this heavy box.
6. The children do .... want to go to the park.

Practice

A Copy the sentences below. Underline the **negative** words.
Write the sentences again so that they have the opposite meaning.

1. The woman knew nothing about the accident.
2. He did not have a ticket to get in.
3. The boys had nowhere to go.
4. "I haven't fed the cat," said Dad.
5. They won't go into town.

Extension

A Write the **contractions** of these **negative** words.

1. cannot
2. will not
3. shall not
4. must not
5. have not
6. should not
7. would not
8. does not
9. do not
10. is not
11. could not
12. has not

B These sentences have two negative words.
They do not mean what the writer wanted them to mean.
Write each sentence again so that it means what the writer wanted.
The first one is done for you.

1. I wanted to win the race but I didn't have no luck.
   I wanted to win the race but I didn't have any luck.
2. Pam didn't want to go nowhere.
3. I mustn't throw nothing away.
4. Mum will not get no bus today.
5. I don't want no beans for tea.

Unit 26 Nouns

There are different types of **nouns**. Most nouns are the names of things you can see and touch.

There are **common nouns**.

a **camera**

There are **proper nouns**.

Mr Jones

There are **collective nouns**.

a **shoal** of fish

There are **compound nouns**.

a **notebook**

Abstract nouns are the names of things you cannot touch, taste, smell or hear. They are the names of qualities, feelings and times:

qualities	bravery	heroism	stupidity
feelings	fear	happiness	anger
times	evening	Wednesday	holiday

Focus

A Say what type of **noun** each of these is.

1. horse
2. bunch
3. raindrop
4. box
5. Sally
6. football
7. herd
8. farmer

B Write the seven **abstract nouns** from the box.

| creature | kindness | picture | station | Friday | sun |
| cottage | wisdom | freedom | happiness | poverty | fear |

Practice

Copy the sentences below. Underline the **common noun** and the **abstract noun** in each sentence.

1. The people admired his talent.
2. That book gave me great pleasure.
3. The old woman lived in poverty.
4. The boy had a happy childhood.

Extension

Abstract nouns can be made from **common nouns**.

Common noun	Abstract noun
robber	robbery
hero	heroism

Abstract nouns can be made from **adjectives**.

Adjective	Abstract noun
kind	kindness
stupid	stupidity

Abstract nouns can be made from **verbs**.

Verb	Abstract noun
to please	pleasure
to encourage	encouragement

A Copy the common nouns. Write the abstract nouns that can be made from them.
1. infant 2. friend 3. thief 4. shrub

B Copy the adjectives. Write the abstract nouns that can be made from them.
1. still 2. famous 3. active 4. sad

C Copy the verbs. Write the abstract nouns that can be made from them.
1. to suspect 2. to free 3. to hate 4. to amend

Check-up 3

Nouns

A Write these film titles correctly.

1. the lion king
2. harry potter
3. star wars
4. toy story

B Write a **collective noun** for each of these.

1. soldiers
2. flowers
3. books
4. fish
5. lions
6. birds
7. musicians
8. sheep

C Choose a **noun** from the box on the left and another from the box on the right. Put them together to make a **compound noun**.

| rain   fire   sun   sea   day | shade   light   fighter   drop   shore |

D Copy the sentences below.
Add an **apostrophe** to the owner or owners.

1. The giraffes neck is long and thin.
2. Birds feathers help them to fly.

E Copy the sentences below. Underline the **abstract nouns**.

1. The pain in my arm made me cry.
2. The escape was planned for midnight.
3. It is a mystery where that book has gone.

F Use these abstract nouns in sentences of your own.

1. wisdom
2. misery
3. pain
4. joy
5. generosity

Adjectives

A Copy the sentences below. Underline the **number order adjectives**.

1. Men landed on the moon in the twentieth century.
2. This is the second time I have warned you.
3. He came fifth in the race.
4. We go on holiday on the twenty-second of June.

B Write the **comparative** and **superlative** of each of these adjectives.

1. loud
2. bad
3. shabby
4. good
5. tidy
6. little
7. much
8. kind
9. many
10. some

Singular and plural

Write the **plurals** of these nouns.

1. pony
2. foot
3. loaf
4. piano
5. donkey
6. baby
7. banjo
8. half
9. wharf
10. scarf
11. berry
12. tooth

Prepositions

Copy the sentences below.
Underline the **preposition** in each sentence.

1. The rat hid behind the shed.
2. She threw the ball over the fence.
3. I went into the shop to buy some bread.
4. The tree was growing near the water.
5. I stood between Mum and Dad.

Sentences

A Copy the sentences below.
Underline the **subject** in each sentence.

1. This door needs painting.
2. I have hurt my leg.
3. Some people live on boats.
4. The storm frightened the animals.
5. The noisy children were chasing each other.

B Copy the sentences below.
Underline the **object** in each sentence.

1. I want a banana.
2. The umbrella kept off the rain.
3. The boy kicked the ball.
4. We need to mend the gate.
5. The teacher gave out the books.

C Add interesting **predicates** to complete these sentences.

1. The lonely man _____
2. Every flower _____
3. The two goats _____
4. These torn curtains _____

D Copy the sentences below.
Add the missing punctuation.

1. I will carry that for you said Jake
2. Will you come for tea asked Dan
3. Mark said I can't find my jumper
4. Tom shouted Look out

E Write these sentences again so they say what the writer wanted them to say.

1. I did not get no lunch today.
2. He never goes nowhere on Sunday.
3. The boys couldn't find nowhere to play.
4. The cat didn't climb no trees in the park.
5. Can't I not go out today?

Pronouns

Use these **pronouns** in sentences of your own.

1. myself
2. yourself
3. ourselves
4. itself
5. himself
6. herself
7. yourselves
8. themselves

Verbs

A Copy the sentences below. Use the **past continuous tense** – the verb 'to be' and an 'ing' word – instead of the **verb family name** given in the brackets.

1. I (to talk) to my friend when the telephone rang.
2. She (to run) for the bus when she tripped.
3. Ravi (to post) the letter when it began to rain.
4. I did my homework while my brothers (to read) their books.

B Write these sentences in the **future tense**.

1. The candle burned all night.
2. The bells jingled in the wind.
3. The house was built of stone.
4. The cabbage is rotting in the basket.
5. I listen to the radio on Saturday morning.

C Copy and correct these sentences.

1. The children goes to the park to play.
2. Ali find his ball in the long grass.
3. I wants my tea now.
4. Cats likes to drink milk.
5. The pony gallop around the field.

Contractions

Copy the sentences below.
Add **apostrophes** to the contractions.

1. "I cant go out this evening," said Gita.
2. "We wont be there in time if we dont hurry," said Mum.
3. "You mustnt leave your book at home again," said the teacher.
4. "Why shouldnt you cross the road here?" asked the policeman.
5. "I couldnt win the race," said Jake.